First Classics

Edited and arranged for easy piano by

Frank Metis

GW01418858

Foreword

The German philosopher Goethe once wrote, "If I accept you as you are, I will make you worse; however, if I treat you as though you are what you are capable of becoming, I will help you become that." Accordingly, I have designed this series of publications to help you grow as a musician, and to enhance your playing skills as well as broaden your musical horizons. To help you along this path, I have included within these pages various degrees of "easy" arrangements and compositions, together with entertaining, informative, and witty comments and quotations.

To encourage you to pianistically "go public," pages 28 through 31 include a special Recital Solo. Practice it, and you will surely please your family and friends—and garner some well-deserved applause. To further your creative skills, complete the exercise in the Creative Corner on page 32. It's fun to do, and you'll be on the road to writing your own music! Above all, don't be apologetic about being an "amateur musician" or "butterfingers pianist." All artists begin as students—and the great ones remain students! With perseverance, you can attain the musical heights to which you aspire. There is an inspiring story about Benny Goodman, the great jazz clarinetist, and Frank Sinatra, the legendary pop singer. Many years ago, they appeared together in the old Paramount Theater in New York City. Early one morning, Sinatra arrived at the theater and heard Goodman practicing furiously in the basement. "I don't understand you, Benny," he said to Goodman. "You play so great, why do you practice so hard?" Goodman looked at him coldly and replied, "If I didn't practice, I'd only be good!"Take a lesson from Benny—and some of your own musical favorites: All the great ones practice constantly and learn continually—and all of them started off with "easy" folios like this one! I want to express profound appreciation to my outstanding editor Peter Pickow for his assistance in putting these publications together, conceptually and musically. His enormous knowledge and insightful suggestions, always rendered with unfailing courtesy and good humor, managed to track all of my "unguided missiles" and rescue me from foolish ideas. Also, a hug to my son Gregg Metis for coming up with the title for this series.

It has been said that "music washes away from the soul the dust of everyday life." I hope that these pages will help you to do just that. And, may you enjoy having these selections "at your fingertips."

AMSCO PUBLICATIONS
New York/London/Sydney

Foreword

Front cover illustration: Musical Evening, Johann Strauss by Franz von Bayros

This book Copyright © 1996 Amsco Publications,
A Division of Music Sales Corporation, New York

Order No. AM 92886
US International Standard Book Number: 0.8256.1465.1
UK International Standard Book Number: 0.7119.4961.1

Exclusive Distributors:
Music Sales Corporation
257 Park Avenue South, New York, NY 10010 USA
Music Sales Limited
8/9 Frith Street, London W1V 5TZ England
Music Sales Pty. Limited
120 Rothschild Avenue, Rosebery, Sydney, NSW 2018 Australia

Printed in the United States of America by
Vicks Lithograph and Printing Corporation

[Refusing to give metronome markings] Idiot! Do you
think I want to hear my music always played at the same speed?
Johannes Brahms

Gaudeamus Igitur
from The Academic Festival Overture

Johannes Brahms
(1833–1897)

Maestoso

allargando

[Speaking to a violinist who complained about the difficulty of a certain passage] When I composed that, I was conscious of being inspired by God Almighty. Do you think I can consider your puny little fiddle as He speaks to me?
Ludwig van Beethoven

Für Elise

Ludwig van Beethoven
(1770–1827)

Andante con moto

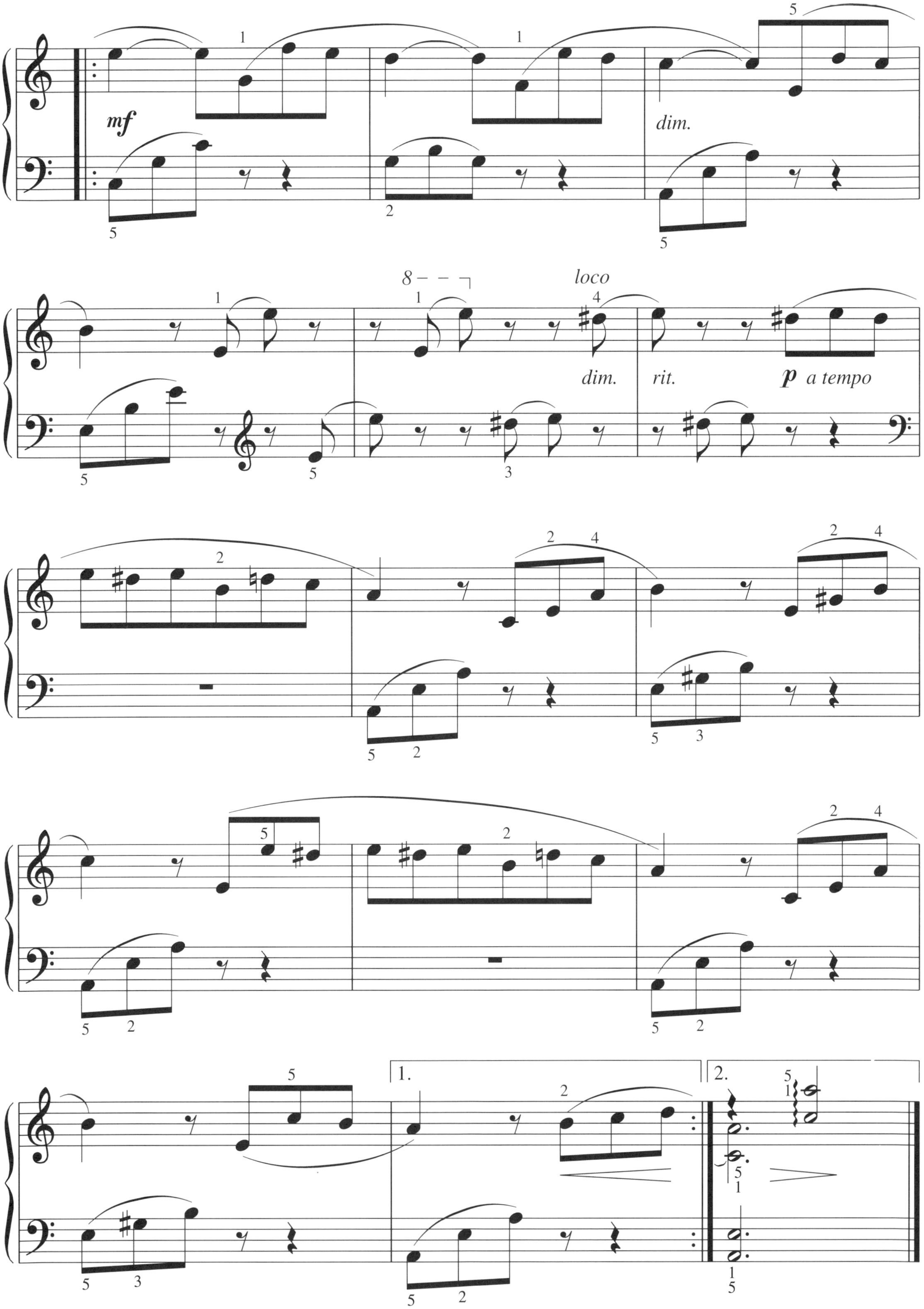
mf
dim.
8
loco
dim.
rit.
p a tempo
1.
2.

[To a singer who had threatened to jump on Handel's harpsichord]
Let me know when you will do that and I will advertise it. For I am
sure more people will come to see you jump than to hear you sing!
George Frideric Handel

Sarabande
from Suite XI

George Frideric Handel
(1685–1759)

Andante con moto

Danse des Mirlitons
from The Nutcracker

Peter Ilyich Tchaikovsky
(1840–1893)

7

In an age of neurathenics, music, like everything else, must be
a stimulant, must be alcoholic, aphrodisiac, or it is no good.
Frederick Delius

Themes
from La Calinda (Koanga)

Frederick Delius
(1862–1934)

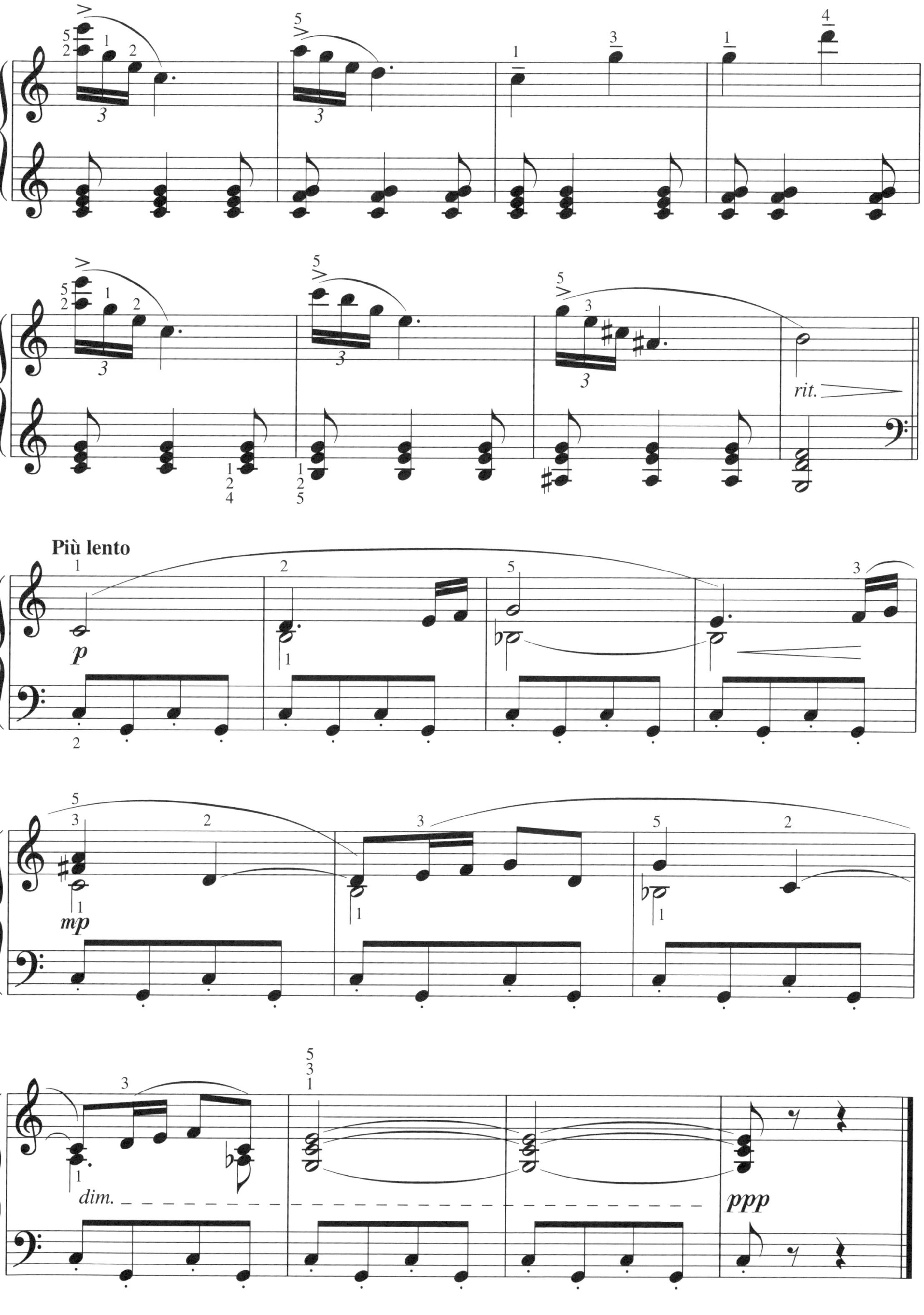
rit.
Più lento
p
mp
dim.
ppp

[On composing overtures] Wait until the evening before opening night.
Nothing primes inspiration more than necessity, whether it be the presence
of a copyist waiting for your work or the prodding of an impresario tearing
his hair. In my time, all the impresarios in Italy were bald at thirty!

Gioacchino Rossini

Theme *from* The Barber of Seville

Gioacchino Rossini
(1792–1868)

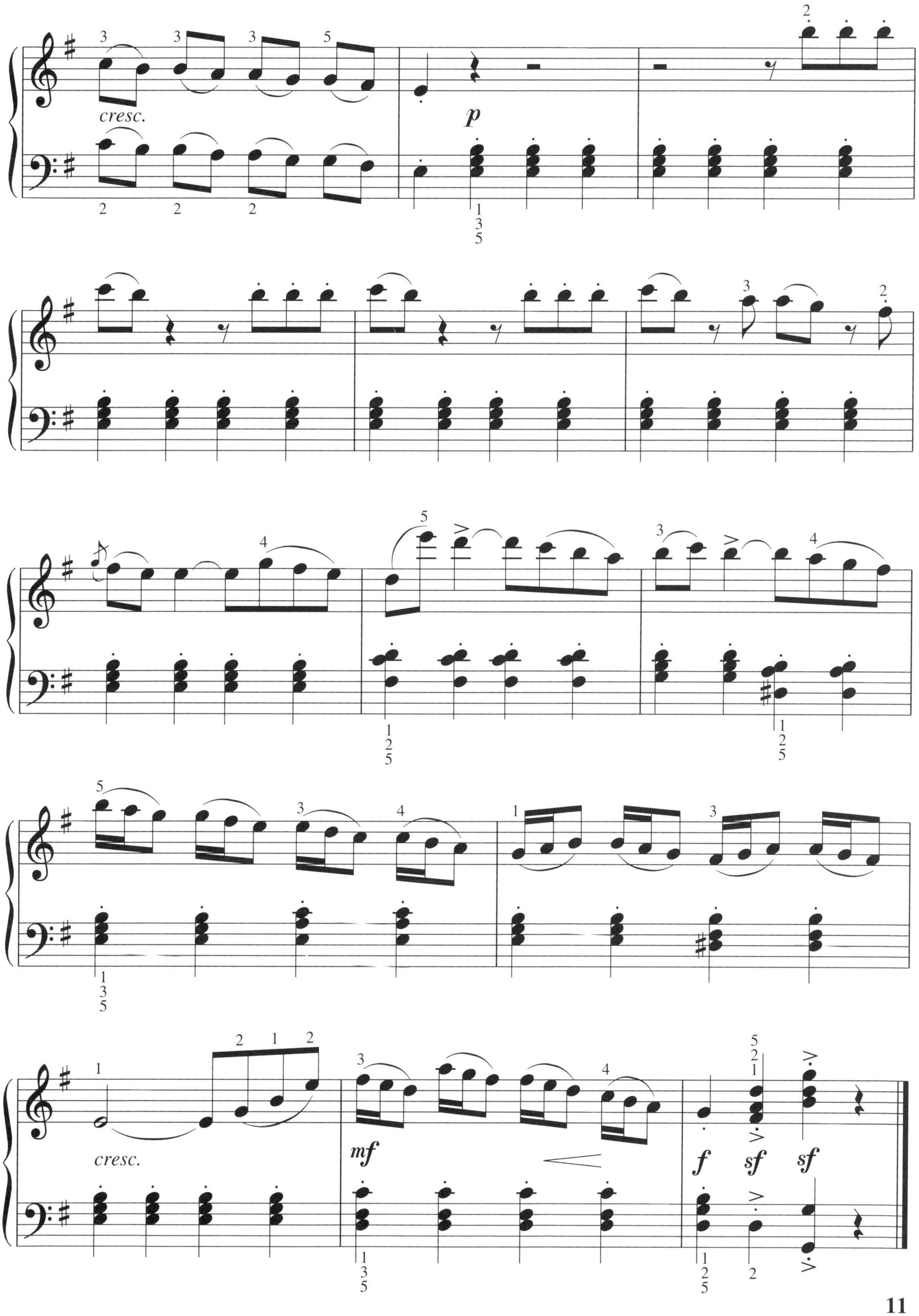
cresc.
p
cresc.
mf
f
sf
sf

Grieg's Peer Gynt music... consists of two or three catchpenny phrases served up with plenty of orchestral sugar.
George Bernhard Shaw

Theme *from* Anitra's Dance
Peer Gynt Suite No. 1

Edvard Grieg
(1843–1907)

After playing Chopin, I feel as if I had been weeping over sins that
I never committed, and mourning over tragedies that were not my own!
Oscar Wilde

Prelude
Opus 28, No. 7

Frédéric Chopin
(1810–1849)

If Bach continues to play in this way, the organ will be
ruined in two years, or most of the congregation will be deaf.
Member of the Arnstadt Council, 1705

Arioso

Johann Sebastian Bach
(1685–1750)

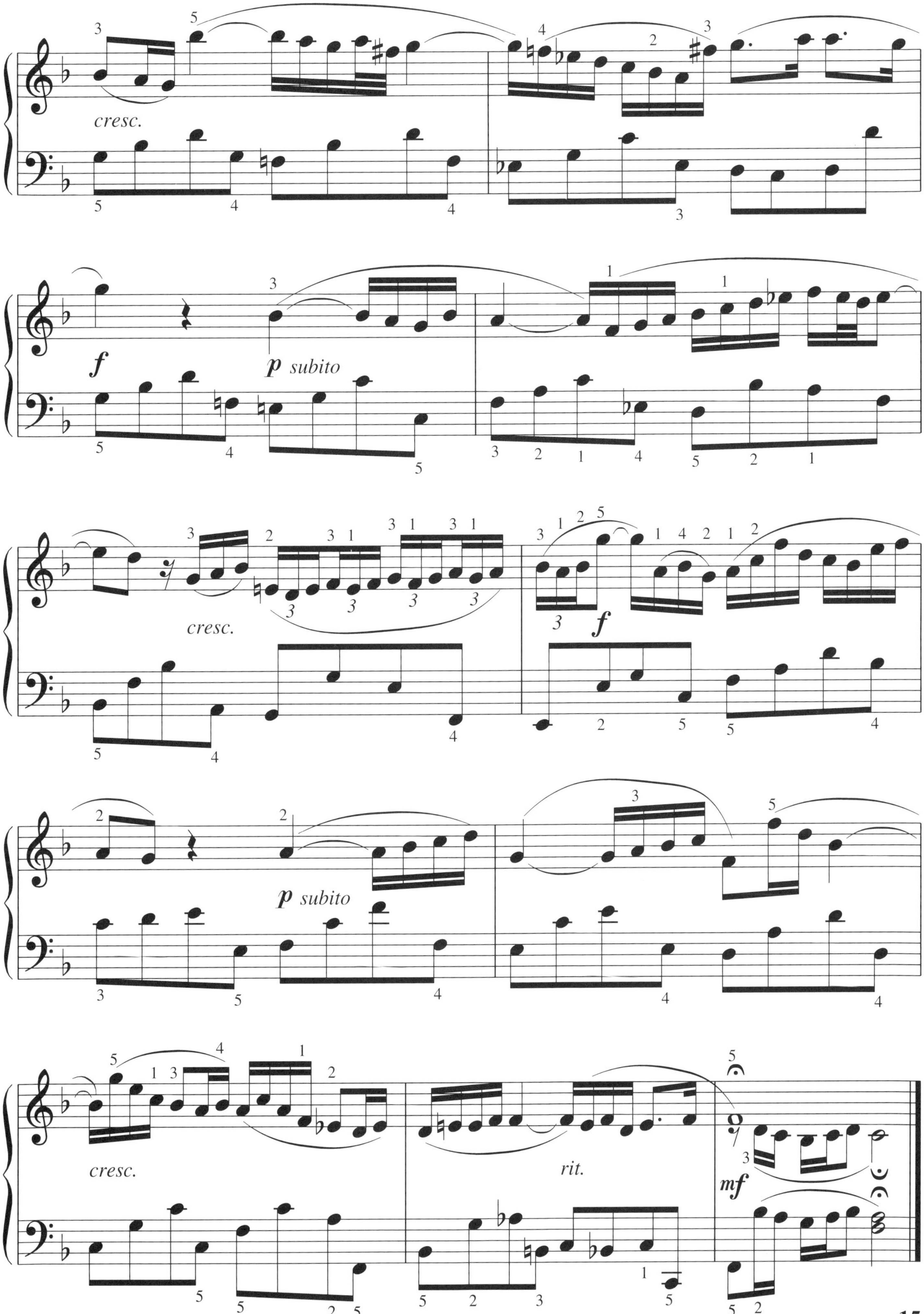
cresc.
f
p subito
cresc.
f
p subito
cresc.
rit.
mf

The attraction of the virtuoso for the public is very
like that of the circus for the crowd. There is always
the hope that something dangerous will happen.
Claude Debussy

Clair de Lune

Claude Debussy
(1862–1918)

Andante très expressif

pp *sempre molto legato*

To next strain — *Fine* —

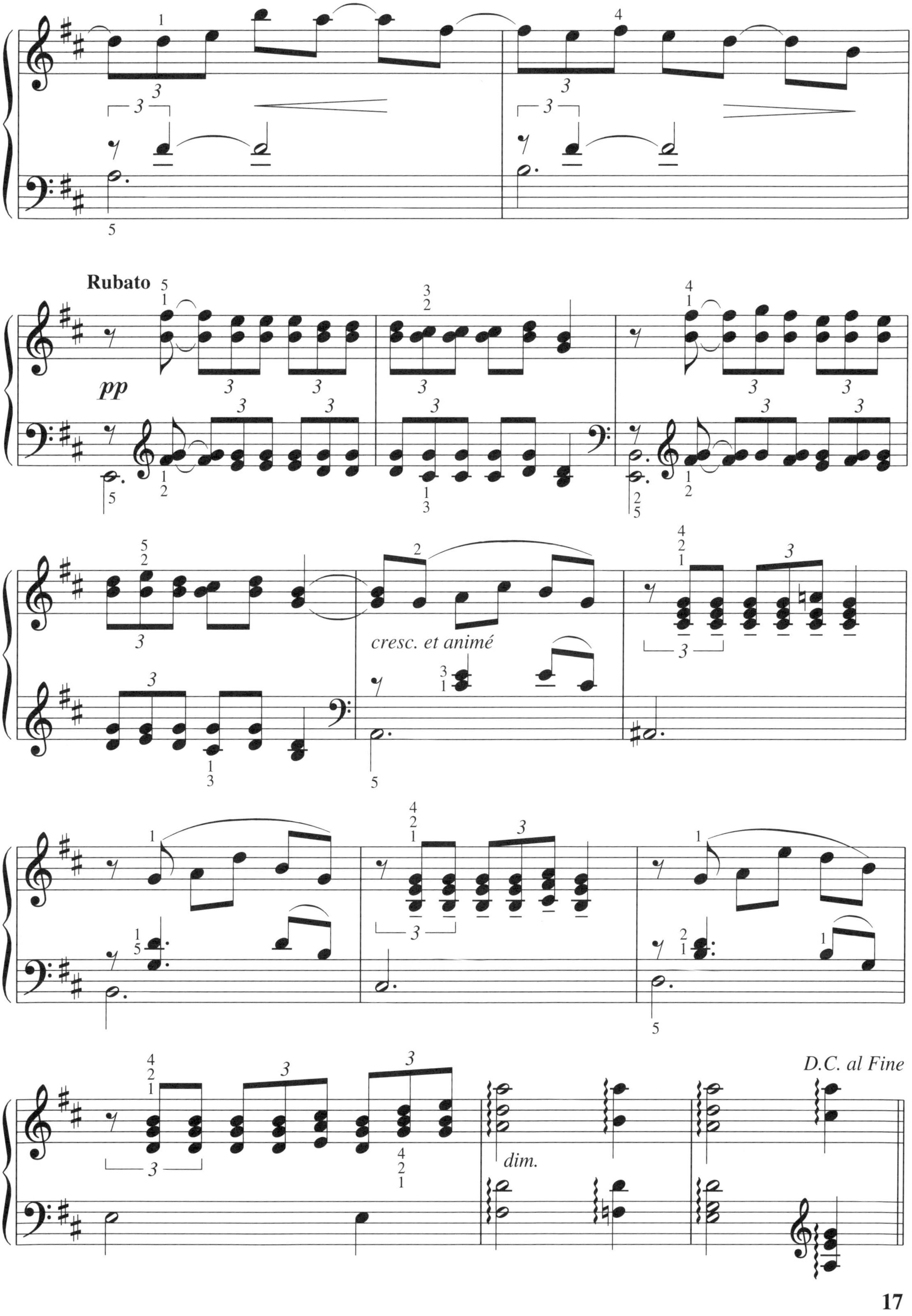
Rubato
pp
cresc. et animé
D.C. al Fine
dim.

As a musician, I tell you that if you were to suppress adultery, fanaticism, crime, evil, the supernatural, there would no longer be the means for writing one note.

Georges Bizet

Themes
from Carmen

Georges Bizet
(1838–1875)

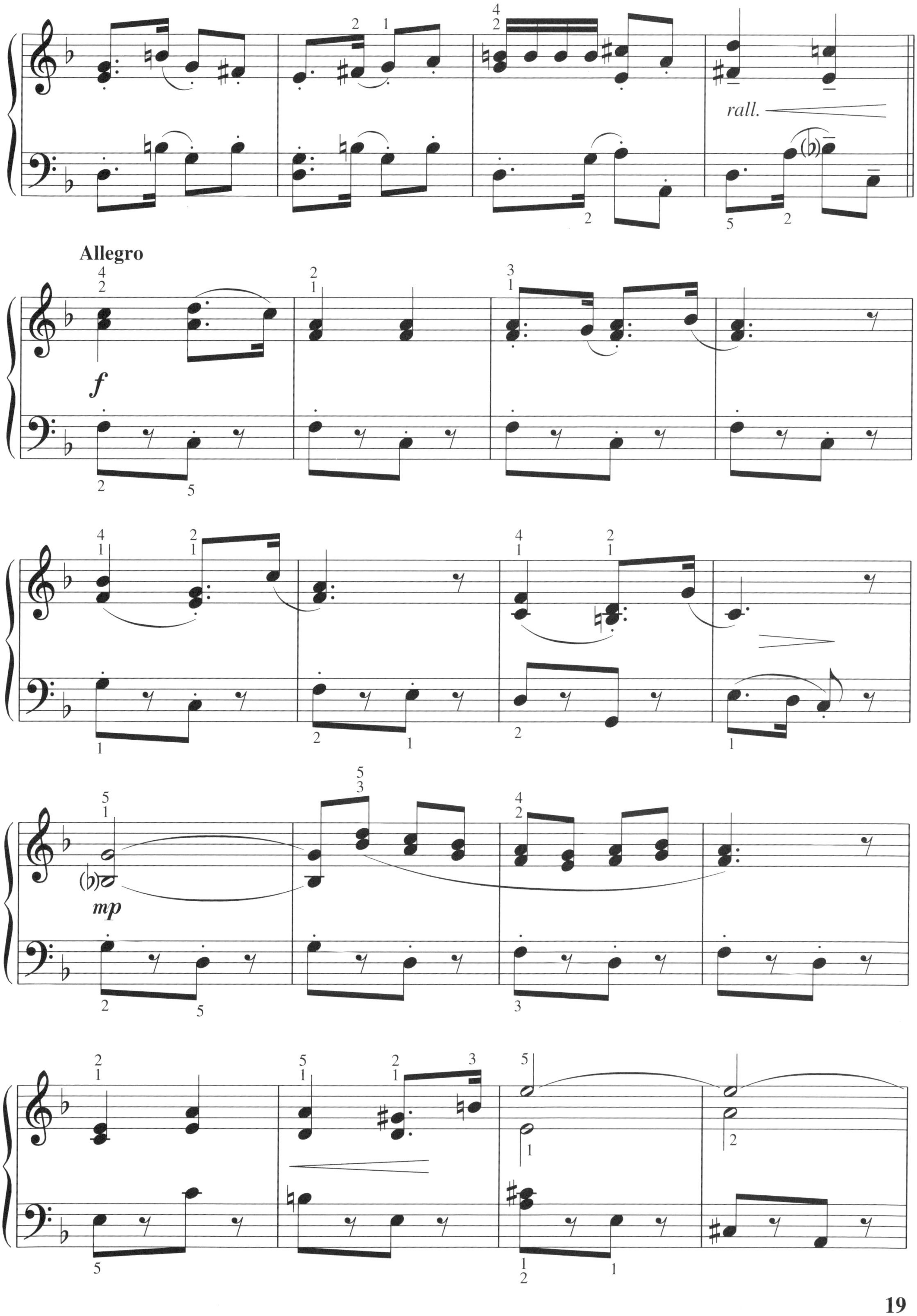
rall.
Allegro
f
mp

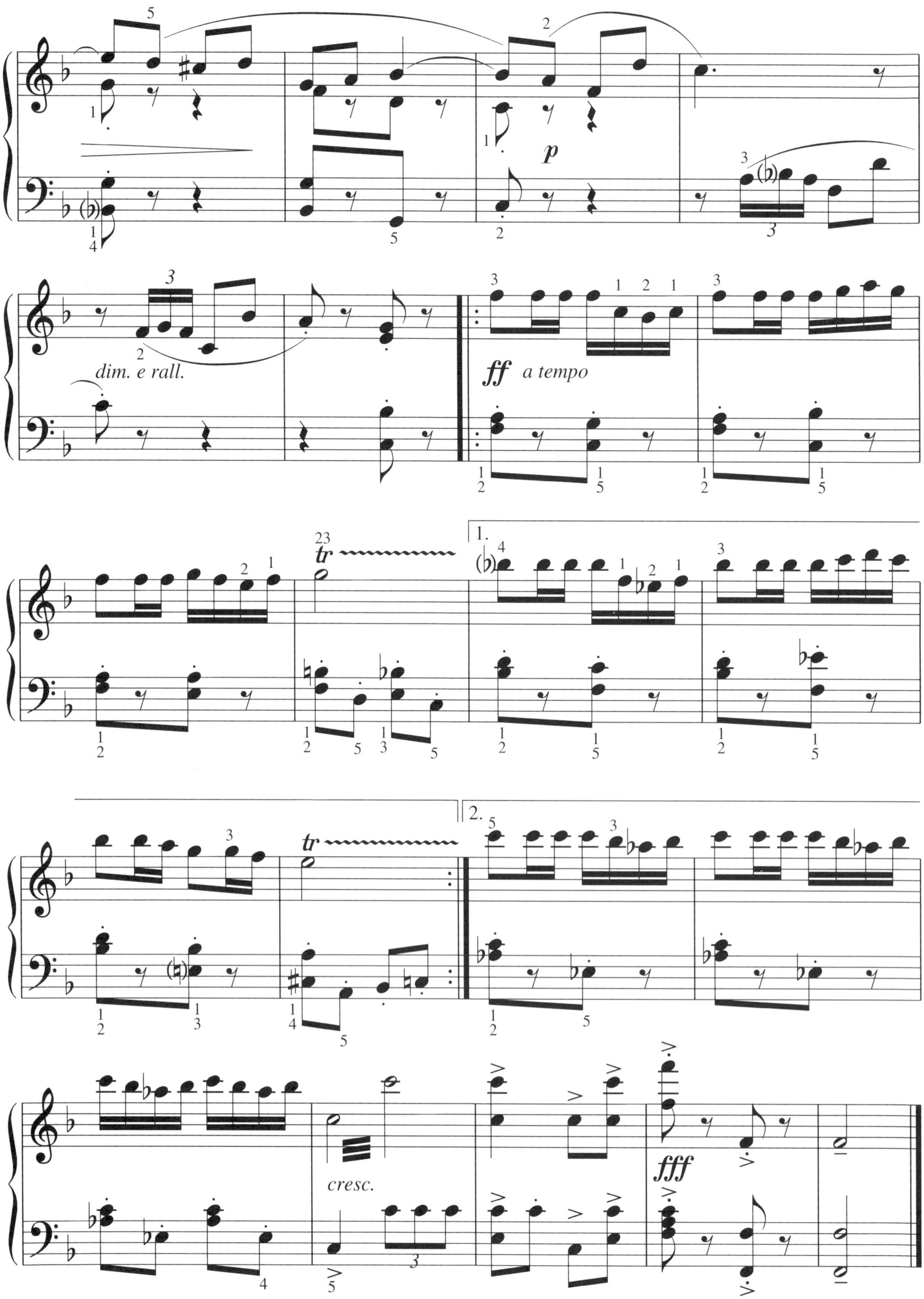
p
dim. e rall.
ff
a tempo
tr
1.
2.
cresc.
fff

Much is to be learned from singers male and female.
But do not believe all they tell you.

Robert Schumann

Melody

Robert Schumann
(1810–1856)

Offenbach's music is wicked. It is abandoned stuff; every accent is a snap of the fingers in the face of moral responsibility.

George Bernard Shaw

Can-Can

from Orpheus in the Underworld

Jacques Offenbach
(1819–1880)

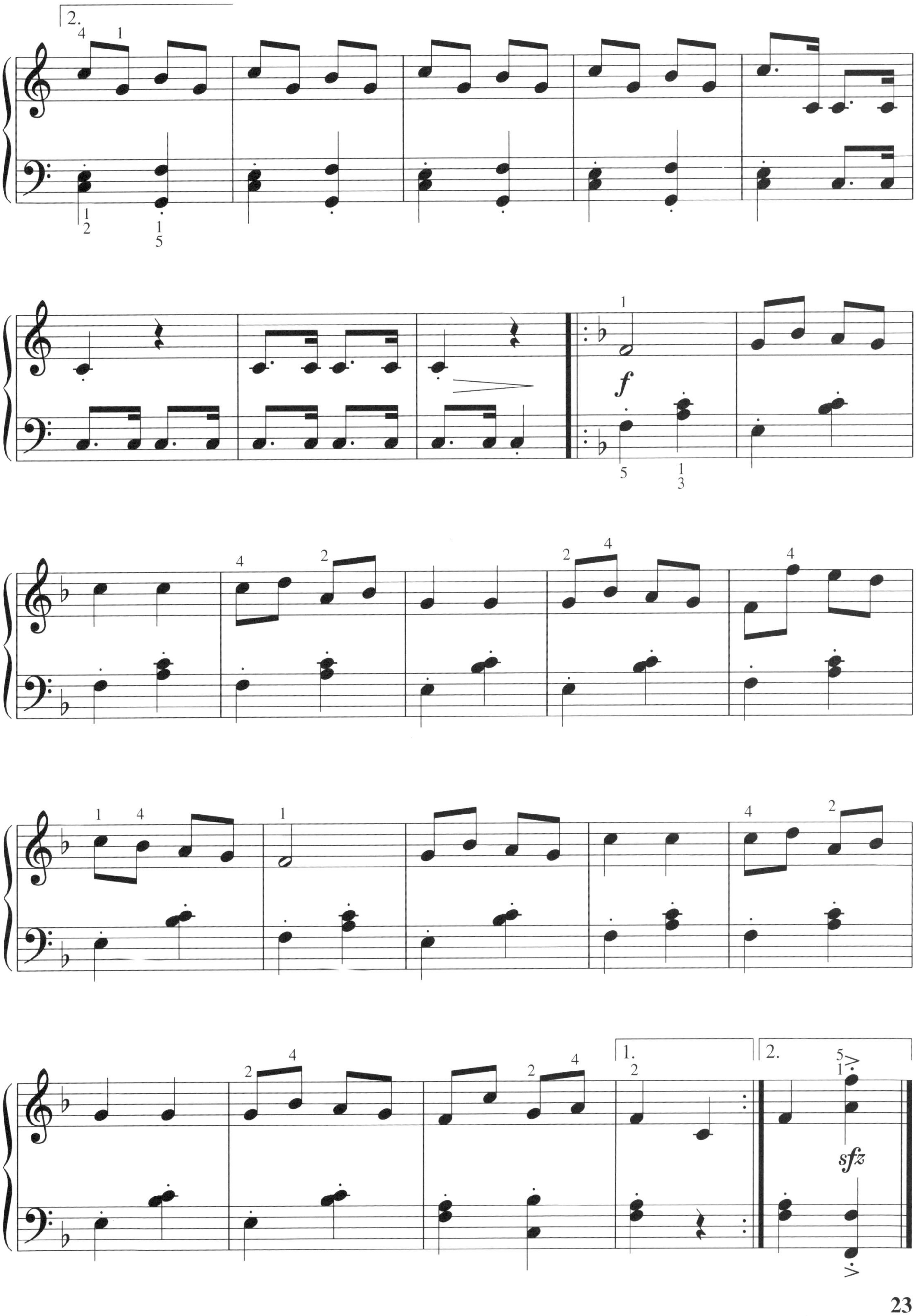
2.
f
1.
2.
sfz

Land of Hope and Glory

Theme from Pomp and Circumstance Military March No. 1

Edward Elgar
(1857–1934)

*Franz Liszt came... but he frightened us. His hair was so long,
and he had such a wild appearance, that when he played
the pianoforte, we were always glad to leave the room.*
Willert Beale

Short Etude

Franz Liszt
(1811–1886)

Andantino

p

semplice e espressivo

un poco cresc. e accel.

mf

un poco ritenuto

più ritenuto e dim.

smorz.

pp

25

[To the composer of music for Meyerbeer's funeral]
Would it not have been better if you had died and
Meyerbeer had written your funeral march?
                              Gioacchino Rossini

Theme *from Coronation March*

from Le Prophète

Giacomo Meyerbeer
(1791–1864)

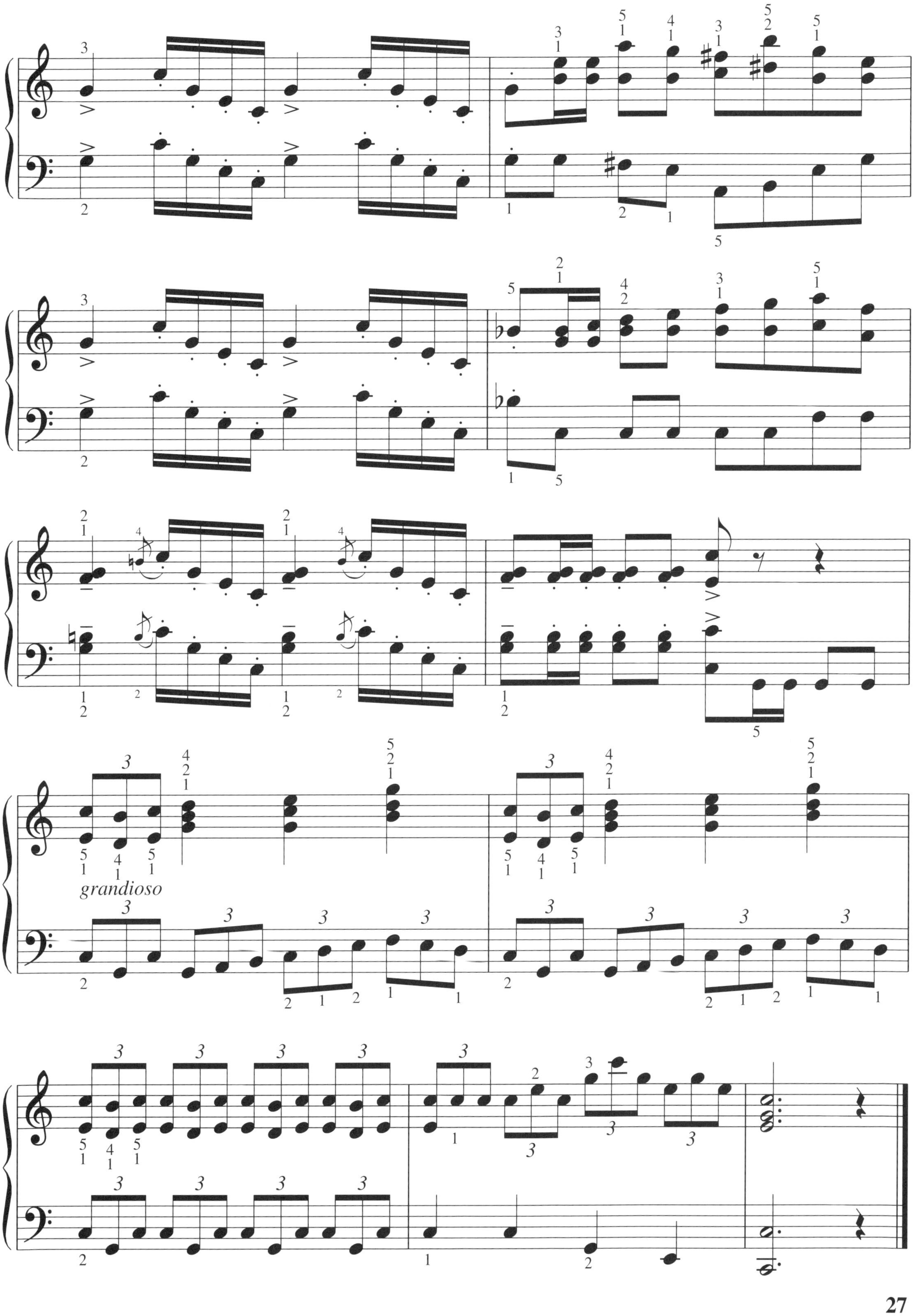
grandioso

Nothing soothes me more after a long and maddening pianoforte recital than to have my teeth drilled by a finely skilled hand.

George Bernard Shaw

RECITAL SOLO

From Rags to Richard…
Wagner, that is!!

(Includes themes from **Tannhäuser, The Flying Dutchman***, and* **Lohengrin.***)*

by Frank Metis

Somewhat frantic, frenzied and frenetic (♩ = 132 plus?)

mp grazioso
mf
mp
f subito
mp subito
f
mp subito
mf
cantabile
melody

melody
cresc. poco a poco
f cresc. poco a poco
ff dim. poco a poco
mf
quasi maestoso

marcato
cresc. poco a poco
f
cresc.
ff
Ped.
rall.
fff a tempo
8
sffz

Only those who attempt the absurd achieve the impossible.
                                        Anonymous

THE CREATIVE CORNER! From "The Pirates of Penzance" by Arthur Sullivan (1842–1900), here is a little waltz - without the melody. Never mind Mr. Gilbert - here is your chance to become Arthur's partner by adding your own melody! Write it in pencil, also select a suitable title!

Title: _____

by _____
and Arthur Sullivan